LEVI FOREST

HOME COOKING FOR YOUR DOG

The Ultimate Guide to Healthy Homemade Dog Food, Learn How to Make Sure to Provide a Healthy, Well-Balanced and Nutritious Food For Your Dog

Descrierea CIP a Bibliotecii Naționale a României
LEVI FOREST
   HOME COOKING FOR YOUR DOG. The Ultimate Guide to Healthy Homemade Dog Food, Learn How to Make Sure to Provide a Healthy, Well-Balanced and Nutritious Food For Your Dog / Levi Forest – Bucharest: Editura My Ebook, 2021
   ISBN

LEVI FOREST

HOME COOKING FOR YOUR DOG
The Ultimate Guide to Healthy Homemade Dog Food,
Learn How to Make Sure to Provide a Healthy,
Well-Balanced and Nutritious Food For Your Dog

My Ebook Publishing House
Bucharest, 2021

TABLE OF CONTENTS

INTRODUCTION 7

Chapter 1. Feeding Your Dog 9

Chapter 2. Homemade Dog Food, Is It Any Good? …... 22

Chapter 3. Homemade versus Store-Bought Dog Food: Which Is Better? 34

Chapter 4. Homemade Dog Food and Treats Recipes ... 45

Chapter 5. Food Dogs Can and Can't Eat 55

CONCLUSION 67

INTRODUCTION

Choosing the right kind of dog food you provide is probably the most critical decision you'll ever make for your dog- puppy or senior. Dog food nutrition without delay impacts every facet of your dog's life. Aspects such as how pups grow, their behavior practices, health, overall well-being and physical appearance are all tightly linked to the nutrition dog owners provide. Needless to say, this is an enormous responsibility.

The Key Benefits of a Healthy, Well-balanced and Nutritious Dog Food Plan

A nutritious well-balanced dog food diet plan encourages:

- Healthy skin and coat
- Strong muscles and well developed bones
- Bright, clear eyes
- More solid stool
- Good dental health
- Less digestive upsets
- Burst of energy

- Few (if any) behavior problems
- Great dog lifestyle
- Long life

Pretty much everything, right?

Homemade Dog Food

Considering the latest news concerning the dog food recall and associated issues with commercial dog foods, the homemade dog food alternative has really come to the forefront.

Planning and preparing your dog's meals from scratch has numerous benefits, which includes the full control of all meals served. You know precisely what goes into every meal and where the produce and ingredients were sourced. In addition to knowing that it has been prepared in clean surroundings.

It does require an organized person to put together a homemade feeding plan and then make all of the everyday dog meals. Common homemade dog meals include big meaty stews, healthy soups, veggies and perhaps some raw bones from time to time. The homemade dog food alternative also has the added responsibility of making nutritionally balanced meals, and achieving the calorie demands for your dog. If you arm yourself with the right dog food recipes, vet's approval and get into a program, this practice isn't all that hard to keep.

CHAPTER ONE

FEEDING YOUR DOG

To sustain your dog's good health condition, it's vital to feed him a well-balanced diet and the correct amount of it every day. There is a wide variety of canine foods available, so it can be hard deciding which selection or make is the most beneficial choice for your pet. There are, however, particular dietary nutrients that a dog can't do without - protein, carbohydrates, fat, vitamins, minerals, fiber, and water -, in addition to age, health and lifestyle factors to consider, and this helps to make the task of picking out the most suitable diet less difficult.

Diet Plan

Dogs are omnivorous in the feeding habits and can be kept satisfactory on specially designed vegetarian diet programs, although they do prefer meat-based meals. In a wild state the dog hunts, kills, feeds, then rests. He may stuff himself on a whole animal one day, and then go without food for the following two or three; this is why a lot of dogs are keen to eat until they're fit to burst - intuition tells them they may have to hold out some time before their next mealtime.

Adult domestic dogs are often fed once a day, but dividing that feed into two meals adds relationship and interest. It's also preferable to feed certain deep-chested breeds, like German Shepherds, Great Danes, and Setters, several small meals as opposed to one big one, to avoid potentially terminal digestive conditions such as bloat.

You will find retail produced clinical diets available, typically only obtainable from veterinarians, that can assist dogs struggling with a wide range of disease, like kidney stones, signs of senility, obesity, digestive disturbances, diabetes, mellitus and tooth and gum problems. There are even food items engineered for long-coated breeds, in addition to life-stage formulas. You may also choose from holistic diets that incorporate no synthetic additives and diets designed for allergy sufferers.

Required Nutrients

Usually, dogs aren't difficult to feed, and they thrive on a diet not really different to humans, albeit with a little more protein. The majority of foods of animal origin, cereal products, root vegetables and fats are easy for them to break down. The trick of correct feeding is to give a balanced diet that provides all essential goodness in the appropriate proportions to one another with the objective intended - work, breeding, growth or health adulthood. These types of nutrients are listed below:

Carbohydrates

Carbohydrates, by means of cooked cereal starch or sugar, provides up to 70% by weight of the dog's food (after taking away any water present) or about two-thirds of the calories. Dog biscuits, pasta and rice are three useful energy foods for dogs, and rice is a useful food item for canines allergic to wheat.

Proteins

Proteins within meat and plants (although the latter is substandard to the former) improve body tissue, carry out "repairs" and produce hormones. The dry matter of dog food ought to contain at least 15% protein, of which the majority should come from animal foods (meat and dairy products), or high-quality vegetable protein like soya.

Minerals

Minerals are occasionally referred to as "ash" on dog-food labels. The essential ones are calcium, phosphorus and sodium chloride (common salt) in a well balanced combination. Calcium and phosphorus constitute most of the mineral matter of bone and must be utilized at the rate of about 3% calcium/phosphorus in the diet; an excessive amount of calcium in the diet, particularly in large-breed puppies, can result in skeletal irregularities, while an excessive amount of phosphorus (found in high meat and offal diets) could potentially cause eclampsia in lactating female dogs.

Additional essential minerals for good health, like zinc and copper, occur naturally in meat, cereals as well as other components of a balanced diet.

Vitamins

Vitamin A (also called retinol) is important for growth and eyesight, while vitamins of the B group are crucial for the upkeep, in particular, of the nervous system.

Vitamin D assists the body create calcium, required for healthy bones and teeth, as is phosphorus. Vitamin E (tocopherol) is important for the leveling of cell membranes.

Since canines can create their own vitamin C (ascorbic acid, essential for maintaining healthy connective tissue and skin), this doesn't necessarily have to be part of the diet.

Fat

Fat contributes to food palatability, but is in fact only essential as a source of the essential fatty acids (EFAs, also known as polyunsaturates) which are vital to maintain body health. They work mainly by handling water loss through the skin. A deficiency in EFAs can lead to reproductive, skin, coat and wound therapeutic problems.

Fiber

An absence of fiber in the diet may result - particularly in elderly, inactive dogs - in bowel problems and other digestive problems cause by sluggish bowels. Fiber is provided through the indigestible plant matter in foods like cooked and raw veggies as well as cereals.

Balancing Act

It's critical that the balance of nutrients provided to a dog is correct, since excesses could cause as many health issues as inadequacies. If your dog gets more calories each day than his body requires, he will get fat. Just as in humans, obesity accounts for many canine illnesses, like heart problems, joint ailments and decline in lung function.

Just How Much Must I Feed to My Dog?

This relies on your pet's:
- Size
- Activity level
- Age
- Personality
- Temperature of surroundings

Young puppies and those being worked, or which are really active every day, may require more food (calories) per day than the average pooch, while an old, inactive dog will need less.

Keeping Track of the Calories

Energy is calculated in units of heat called calories. In a healthy dog, the amount of calories he requires levels out the number of calories that his body uses daily. If this balance is well kept, the dog stays healthy and fit and his weight remains regular. An underfed dog steadily loses weight and condition as his body pulls on the reserves of fat and protein to make up the insufficiencies in his diet.

The amount of calories a dog needs daily is dependent on his size, life stage, activity level and individuality. As an example, a little healthy adult dog with two hours of regular activity a day demands anything between 125 and 700 calories daily depending on his size; a big dog will need from 1,400 per day, depending on size.

Puppies require more calories with regards to their body weight since they're growing swiftly, tend to be more susceptible to heat loss because of their small size, and their energy requirements are greater. Lactating female dogs require some 50 to 60% more calories than usual, and highly active (working) dogs require at least 40% more calories than normal moderately energetic requirements.

When Should I Feed My Dog?

Most owners feed either in the morning or the evening, and quite often both, determined by their dog's age needs or individual preferences. Some canines fare better with their daily ration broken into two or even three meals, while some are pleased to eat their daily allowance in just a single helping, providing it's safe for them to do so.

It's best to not feed adult dogs at the same periods each day, since counting on a rigid routine can upset the dog if you come home late and aren't able to give him food at the predicted time. Being unsure of when it will be fed likewise helps feed a dog food-orientated, which often proves most helpful when training; additionally, it discourages fussy eating.

Feeding Recommendations

Here are a few basic guidelines to adhere to when feeding your dog.

- Place a feeding mat, or newspaper, under feeding bowls, since many canines aresloppy eaters.
- It is advisable to introduce changes to diet little by little to prevent intestinalproblems.
- Never give spiced food or that to which any liquor has been added
- To avoid choking, get rid of all bones from fresh meats and fish.
- Fresh, clean drinking water must always be accessible.
- Make certain food and water bowls are always clean.

- By no means allow your dog to consume chocolate intended for humanconsumption, as it's toxic to them.
- Confer with your vet if your dog exhibits any reluctance to eat or drink.
- Dissuade your dog from begging at the table, and definitely don't give into it.

Food Types

Good-quality proprietary food is the simplest to feed. It consists of all the essential nutrients in the correct proportions, which includes vitamins and minerals that may be lacking from a home-made diet of fresh or cooked meat and table scraps.

These are four forms of commercially prepared food.

1. **Wet or Moist Canned or Pouch Dog Food**

Canned food has high water content, is available in a wide range of flavors and is usually the preferred choice of dogs.

Pros:
- Extremely palatable
- Contains all the nutrients a dog needs
- Long storage time if unopened

Cons:
- Bulky to store and heavy to carry
- Fattening
- Strong odor
- Not good for teeth
- Contains many artificial additives
- Spoils quickly
- Expensive

2. **Semi-moist Pouch Dog Food**

Often containing vegetable protein like soya, this food type contains less water than canned, therefore keeps well in a bowl without drying out and losing texture.

Pros:
- Palatable
- Contains all the nutrients a dog needs
- Easier to store than the cans

Cons:
- Fattening
- Strong odor

- Not good for teeth
- Very expensive
- Contains man-made artificial additives
- Spoils quickly

3. Dry Complete Dog Food

As its name suggests, dry complete food contains minimal water and all the nutrients your dog needs. Some types are designed to be moistened with water before feeding, while other types can be fed as they are, in which case your dog will need plenty of waterto drink in conjunction with it.

Pros:
- Economical
- Low odor
- Contains all the nutrients a dog needs
- Better for teeth
- Convenient to foodCons:
- Bulky to store
- Goes off if stored too long
- Not as palatable as canned/semi-moist
- High cereal content can cause problems for gluten-sensitive dogs

4. **Dry Complementary Dog Food**

Designed to be fed with canned, cooked or raw meat, this food usually comprises cereal meal or biscuits. Fed alone, it doesn't fulfill a dog's daily nutritional needs.

Pros:
- Economical
- Low odor
- Good source of energy
- Most are supplemented with vitamins and minerals
- Better for teeth

Cons:
- Time-consuming to mix with protein-giving ingredients
- Spoils if stored too long
- Bulky to store

Homemade Food

A lot of dogs enjoy homemade foods, but basing a completely balanced diet around these can be really difficult; a vitamin and mineral supplement will likely be needed as well - consult your vet for advice.

For easy feeding, particularly for busy owners, it's simpler to stick to proprietary dog food and only give a periodic homemade meal for a treat, or to tempt a dog that is ill and has lost his appetite. In the case of the latter, items such as cooked porridge, boneless meats and fish, and scrambled eggs are often appreciated and easily digested. Always allow cooked foods to cool before serving.

In the succeeding chapters, we'll focus more on homemade dog food - their pros and cons, and how to make each recipe good and sumptuous for your dog.

CHAPTER TWO

Homemade Dog Food, Is It Any Good?

Ignore the restaurant doggy bag. Nowadays, more dogs are eating their own patios, gulping down homemade canine food. There have been gradual rises in the number of people who are requesting help with creating homemade diets for their canines, according to majority of veterinarians in the US. The trend to homemade dog food started about a decade ago, and the vast majority of dog owners continue to feed their dogs commercial pet foods. The rise for homemade dog food got stronger after the spring 2007 recall of melamine-tainted pet food.

Apart from product contamination scares, numerous pet owners feel that homemademeals are a fresher option to ready-made pet food. There are also pet owners who have considerable time and have a quite strong bond with their pet and feel that if they're going to maintain a healthy diet, they want their dog to eat healthy, as well.

Owners may also prepare and cook for their pets as an expression of affection since most pet owners see their dogs as children.

Balanced Nutrition

So you're lured to try home cooking for your pooch. Exactly what should you take into account?

Whether owners are getting recipes from a guide book, the net, or via their vet or veterinary nutritionist, one issue tops the list. Owners intend to make sure the recipe is going to supply something that is complete and balanced for their dog. From a nutritional perspective, that's the biggest obstacle that someone has when trying to feed homemade. There aren't any magic foods or ingredients for this.

Commercial pet foods are designed to provide sufficient nutrients. But dog owners who make homemade dog food must ensure that the diet includes a protein source, a carbohydrate source, sufficient vitamins and minerals, plus some fat. Dogs do have a necessity for a small sum of fat.

Home cooks can blend protein and carbohydrates in a variety of combinations, such as lamb and rice, beef and potatoes, or chicken and pasta. Carbs are an economical source of energy and supply some important amino acids and fatty acids.

Furthermore, a selection of vegetables would be perfectly suitable, even though vets caution towards onions and garlic, which can be poisonous to dogs.

Additional foods to protect your dogs from: raisins, grapes, macadamia nuts, chocolate, and raw meat, which unearths canines to risks, like salmonella and E. coli. All meat must be cooked properly.

Even though owners can find plentiful recipes for homemade dog food online and in books, some professionals encourage pet owners to take the recipes first to their vet and ask if their pet doctor could help them determine if it's balanced.

Moreover, owners doing homemade diets must have their dog and the diet assessed at least twice a year. Owners also need to remember that dogs in different life stages or with health disorders can have totally different dietary requirements than a normal, healthy adult canine.

Owners can also search for a reputable vet nutritionist to assist them produce a balanced diet. Often, these specialists are available through a close by vet school, or may be open to consult with your regular vet by means of phone or the web.

For pet owners who wish to find dog food recipes online, internet sites that are run by board-certified veterinary nutritionists are good source for recipes.

Supplementation

Do dogs eating homemade dog food require supplementation to make certain they're getting sufficient nutrients? The answer is YES.

Specialists say nutritional inadequacies can result in health issues. Calcium is among the most common deficiency in a homemade diet plan that isn't professionally balanced. When canines don't get adequate calcium, they're vulnerable to a condition known as nutritional secondary hyperparathyroidism, which can result in soft bones and boneinjuries.

Vets have seen these kinds of results on young dogs consuming unbalanced homemade diets. They see issues with their bone growth -- they're clearly not growing normally, thus you'll see bent limbs, or they're really bent and bowed. Sometimes, it may also be serious enough that they see actual broken bones.

Apart from calcium, other vitamins and minerals are crucial, too, such as magnesium, iron, and zinc. These nutrients need to be covered, which can be very tough for homemade dog food.

Canine owners must ask their vets with regard to supplementation.

Time and Cost

Needless to say, it's more time-consuming to cook than to buy commercial dog food at the store. As for expense, a lot will depend on the size of the dog.

Large dogs, for example, Saint Bernard and Rottweiler, are more expensive to feed compared to small breeds. If you have a dog that's over 50 or 60 lbs. -- for instance, you have two or more of them -- obviously, the cost will be more, compared to the owner thathas two tiny Yorkie.

It's also critical that owners keep in mind to stay thorough and strictly follow the suggested dietary formula. A lot of owners, as time passes, will make little alterations in the diet as a result of ease of cooking or price of ingredients, an event known as recipe drift. You should not make these changes without conferring with a vet, as they could trigger malnutrition.

Shelf-life and Storage

Packaged foods have a long shelf-life. Not so with homemade meals. It's an advantage that with homemade food you're opting for fresh ingredients; it's a disadvantage that you don't have a long shelf life.

For small dogs, owners can make a big batch, freeze it, and take out servings as required. This is going to last for some time. But meals for large canines are best kept in the refrigerator since it's most likely going to be gone in just a couple of days.

The important thing: Home-cooked diets can be very healthy and gratifying for owners, but demand a commitment of time and extra cost from the owner, and assessment with a vet to make sure the diet is not causing the dog harm.

Homemade Recipes

Which would you prefer for dinner - a microwaveable TV dinner or a homemade concoction at home? Just about everyone has eaten both, and have a personal preference. Odds are, whoever is making the homemade food can do a lot better than a frozen brick of "food." This situation may make it simpler to empathize with your canine when you fill his bowl with nuggets of processed meal and he looks up your with the facial expression that just about say, *"are you be kidding me?"*

Or perhaps, your furry best friend is more than willing to scarf down anything that gets inhis bowl. If so, you may want to ask yourself, "Is traditional dog food the best thing for him?" Your dinner alternatives may well be a no-brainer, but finding the right option for your pet isn't usually that simple. He's counting on you to make the healthiest, and yes the most pleasurable, selections for him.

When you make food at home for your pet, you're guaranteed that your dog is eating foods that are clear of preservatives, additives, and chemicals that are often present in commercial dog foods. The big question is: is this enough to meet his daily nutritional requirements?

Various Kinds of Homemade Dog Food

Yes, there are. Just like human food, homemade dog food can be classified so as to filter the search for your furry friend's best diet. But, lines may be blurred, and ideas can overlap. For example, you may decide to feed a raw dog food diet while staying away from all of the foods that specialists have deemed possibly damaging. Or you may choose to use holistic health concepts while using all organic and natural ingredients. That is what homemade dog food is centered on, after all - modifying your dog's diet in a mannerthat fulfills you both.

Raw Dog Food or Biologically Appropriate Raw Food (BARF)

Your dog is a wild animal that's been domesticated. And, as with human beings, any species' best diet is its indigenous one. And a dog's native diet is meat. Furthermore, numerous would attest that raw meat is ideal. Unlike human beings, dogs aren't usually prone to conditions lie salmonella and e-coli.

Organic Homemade Dog Food

You'd have to be living under a rock if you've overlooked all of the fuss pertaining to organic foods. An entire bunch of people believe that bug killers, herbicides, human waste, sewage gunge, radiation, genetic changes, and synthetic additives have no place in or on our produce. But how about meat? Are you aware that your meat - and the meat that you prepare for your pet - can be organic and natural, as well?

Organic meat is farmed from animals that have been grown devoid of synthetic growth hormones or medicines, and have not been fed animal by-products. Organic and natural foods provide no more nourishment than conventional ones, but their appeal is strictly about what's NOT inside them. You'll be spending more though for less but, it's muchless of what you don't want and don't need. Most grocery store carry organic meat nowadays so finding them won't be a problem.

Homemade Holistic Dog Food

Holistic feeding approaches and medicine stand upon the concept that feeding the mind and body assists to regain and manage health and vigor. Principles consist of ideals like balance and assortment. Holistic diets may be given raw or cooked - your decision.

Meal rotation and assortment is important to holistic health principles, just like variety is vital to your own good diet regime. Holistic dog food concepts dictate that grains are acceptable for dogs - in line with the premise that when dogs eat wild animals, they likewise ingest the contents of the stomach of those animals, which includes grains and greens. Many holistic dog food recipes are positioned around two parts protein, one part carbohydrates, and one part veggies. Using these guidelines, you are able to create a variety of recipes.

Do Supplements Have A Spot In Your Pup's Diet?

Though views differ significantly, it's a belief of many others that a healthy dog's nutritional specifications can be fulfilled with nothing more than food and exercise. Calcium supplement and Magnesium levels are often the only two deficiency considerations when feeding a homemade dog food recipe diet.

You may boost calcium with unflavored yogurt, white cheese, pulverized egg shells, and sardines. Vitamin D to discharge the calcium can be acquired from cod liver oil or time spent outside, on a sunny day. Magnesium is found kelp and spinach, that are both acceptable, but only when steamed first.

The Unquestionably Healthy Dog

Regardless of feeding principle that you select for your dog, some values encounter little discussion among pros:

- Canines need protein - vegetarian diets are broadly disputed and don't offer complete nutrition for animals that are generally carnivorous.
- Commercial dog foods that include a large portion of grains provide little nutrition.

- Some commercial dog foods include additives and a lot more sinister components, like cancerous tissue, by-products of ill animals, shelter kills, and synthetic ingredients.
- Harmful toxins aren't strangers either.
- Foods that are not good for you are most likely bad for your dog. Fried foods and sugar-laden goodies sabotage other valiant endeavors and provide little if any nourishment.

So, Should You Cook For Your Dog?

Not surprisingly, you may feel stressed out at the notion of feeding your dog from your own kitchen. Perhaps you have little time to cook even for your own human family. Take into account using the following time-saving suggestions to make your dog's improved wellness and longevity achievable:

- Instead of dicing fresh veggies, keep bags of frozen ones readily available.
- Instead of pureeing veggies, make use of prepared baby food.
- Prepare meals ahead of time and freeze in individual helping sizes.
- Eat what your pet eats - make meals that everyone in the family, human and canine can enjoy.

- Strike a deal with your grocer or butcher. Talk to him about what you want, and schedule a specific day of the week when you are able stop by and acquire what he's reserved just for you.
- Use your slow cooker. Put approved ingredients into the slow cooker before goingto work.
- Involve the whole household.
- Use the pleased expression on your pet's face to energize your finding of some extra minutes daily to give him homemade food.

CHAPTER THREE

Homemade versus Store-Bought Dog Food: Which Is Better?

It is essential to decide on the right diet for a dog. This chapter points out the benefits, along with the drawbacks, of homemade food and store-bought food. Is one superior to the other? What are the variations between do-it-yourself and store-bought pet food? Many dog owners have contradictory views with regards to choosing the best food for their pet. These points can help to determine whether homemade food or food purchased from a store is way better for your pet.

Nourishment

Nutrition needs to be your primary concern when selecting the right food for your pet. Store-bought food may appear to be the healthiest, and most reliable option, however, many incorporate preservatives, chemical compounds and additives that aren't healthy for your dog. Don't assume all dog food can is junk, but you must check out the labels cautiously to help you find the right store-bought food for your pet.

Alternatively, homemade dog food doesn't incorporate any chemicals and only contains natural elements. Even so, if you choose to make your own dog food, you must be certain that it meets your dog's nutritional requirements. Both store-bought and homemade pet food can be nutritious but it's your decision which you choose to feed your dog. You must obtain the endorsement of your vet before selecting a diet for your pet.

Assortment

Homemade food has a tendency to offer a greater variety of tastes and flavors than store- bought food. Store-bought pet food generally only is available in a small selection of various flavors. If you would like your dog to savor a diversified diet, you might like to think about homemade food. You'll find recipes for a selection of different dog food and treats on the internet. Your dog will take pleasure in the effort you put into producing new and delicious treats and food for him to chow down.

Management

If you opt to give your dog homemade food, you'll have full control of what your pet eats every day. You can make sure that your pet doesn't eat any potentially dangerous components. If you choose to feed your dog store-bought food, may very well not know exactly what your dog consumes. If control is essential to you when it comes to your dog's diet, a diet of homemade food will be the best choice.

Expense

Is there a variation in cost between store-bought and homemade pet food? Not really. If you decide to purchase high-quality and organic products for your homemade dog food, it'll be costly. If you opt to buy the best, premium brands of dog food in the store, it will likewise be pricey. If you choose your manufacturers or ingredients meticulously, you can lessen the cost of dog food. Above all, you shouldn't bargain the health and well- being of your pet.

It's completely your choice, as the owner, whether you choose to provide your dog homemade or store-bought food. If you opt to make any changes to your dog's present diet, you must ensure that you introduce new foods little by little to avoid diarrhea and digestive difficulties.

Which Is More Cost-Effective: Homemade or Store-Bought Dog Food?

Cooking for yourself is practically always less expensive than buying ready-made food. But, how about for your dog? Whether homemade dog food cost less than store-bought is determined by a couple of elements, like what grade of commercial dog food you purchase and what ingredients you work with to make your homemade dog food.

Processed Dog Food: Canned

The cost per 12-ounce can of dog food varies widely based on the manufacturer. A mid- range brand pet food or store brands charges around $1.25 each can. A normal premium can of dog food costs about $2.50. The price per 16 ounces for basic canned pet food is $1.67, and $3.33 for high quality canned food.

Remember that when you compare dog food rates, you can generally feed your dog a little less of the higher-quality brands and still offer your pet with similar nutrients.

Processed Dog Food: Dry

Yet again, the cost of dry dog food differs a lot with respect to the brand and grade. For midrange dry food, the price per 30-pound bag is about $35. High quality dry dog food averages $65 for a 30-pound bag. So, the cost per pound for dry midrange pet food is $1.17 per pound. The cost per pound for kibble is around $2.17.

Homemade Dog Food: Regular Ingredients

The chances are nearly endless when you're making homemade dog food. The value to make home-cooked dog dinners is determined by the ingredients you decide on and changing rates. Dog food recipes derive from a ratio of three-fifths meat, one-fifth grain and one-fifth veggie.

Homemade Dog Food: Organic Ingredients

You could decide you want to work with organic products in your home cooking to compete with the top-quality dog food brands. The value for organic ingredients is pretty much always higher.

Common Myths and Misconceptions about Homemade Dog Food

It's been a couple of years since the first melamine-related pet food recall, and in the course of that time, more dog lovers than ever decided to turn to homemade diets- cooked or raw-as coverage from potential issues with commercial pet foods. Is homemade dog food really prevention against dangerous canned foods? Sure, it can be, IF it's nutritionally balanced and accounts for your dog's breed, age, weight, activity and overall composition.

To help dog owners who wish to switch to homemade diet for their dogs, here are eight of the most common myths and misconceptions about homemade dog food. Bear in mind though that this applies to adult, healthy canines.

- *Using fresh, balanced foods will, as time passes, meet my pooch's needs if I deviate the diet plan enough.*

There are certain grounds for this perception; fresh produce truly are more bio-available compared to those made with ready-made ingredients. Furthermore, when an owner preps food at home, she is exactly aware what's going into the food. Nevertheless, when examined, even diets depending on balanced, fresh produce can still show up short of a number of nutrients a dog's needs.

Make-up on this by doing research on the actual nutrient requirements of your pooch; what this means is reading through various books, conversing with nutrition experts and vets, and starting to think with respect to both components and nutritional needs.

- *A multi-vitamin put into the meals will take care of any holes.*

The issue here is this: exactly which multi-vitamin do you use? Any un-supplemented home-prepared diet will be short of some nutrients and ample or loaded with others. But since there is no conventional formula for human multi-vitamins and they vary in what they consist of, just throwing one in the dish isn't the solution.

Deciding on an all-purpose multi made particularly for dogs doesn't always solve the issue either. These generally contain surprisingly low levels of nutrients since it's assumed they'll be put into commercial food, and they are unlikely to supply enough supplements to complete a homemade diet.

- *Adding yogurt to my dog's food every day meals can help her get enough calcium.*

Canines need pretty high amounts of calcium, and plain yogurt definitely WON'T make the grade. Unless you wish to put 40 cups of yogurt to your dog's meals every day. Calcium supplement is constantly required if you aren't feeding raw bones.

- *My personal diet is a result of a careful study of human nutrition books, and I just adhere to similar rules with my pet.*

This can be a quite typical assumption however, it is inaccurate. Present dietary guidelines for humans aren't usually well suited for dogs.

- *My doggie had some soft bowels, so reducing down on fiber will fix that.*

Fiber is a crucial dietary element, and the kind of fiber you use matters more than the quantity.

In case your dog has soft bowels on a homemade diet, move to bland meals or trim down the volume of food by about 30 % for a day or so, and look for other signs that might reveal an illness or unwanted organisms. If the issue doesn't clear up within a couple of days, speak to your vet.

- *I make use of a lot of fresh vegetables in my dog's diet since they offer a greatnumber of health benefits.*

Veggies' factor in the dog diet has become a topic of substantial debate. One approach holds that incorporating them is unacceptable, since canines are carnivores and don't needplant matter. Others stress the requirement for both veggies and fruit to improve not just essential vitamins and minerals but also phytochemicals that could shield your pet from disease.

The thing is dogs' systems tend to be more versatile than other animals, and veggies provide a lot when it comes to health advantages. But once again, we're confronted with the all-important concerns, *"How much vegetable and what kind?"* Some veggies have factors that may hinder the absorption of nutrients, yet others contain solanine - an alkaloid that some think worsens inflammation. Work with veggies sensibly: Minimize dark leafy greens. Green beans and carrots are often safe bets, and pumpkin and sweet potatoes are effectively accepted.

- *Canines don't need carbohydrates, and whole grains can be harmful for them.*

Dogs can process adequate glucose from a diet composed of fat and protein alone.

This means is that deficiency of carbohydrates won't result in a recognizable deficit in the manner that an absence of Vitamin C in humans will generate. It doesn't, nonetheless, imply that a carb-free diet is advisable. The best bet is to try to maintain levels consistent so if necessary, you may make changes.

- *A raw food diet is usually better than one that's cooked since canines fed raw don'tget sick.*

Raw diets deviate in type; some look for nutrient balance while some use a "prey model" strategy, which imitates the diet of wolves or wild dogs as strongly as possible. These diets have grown to be massively popular over the past ten years, and to be sure, there are canines that totally thrive on them. However, some don't. As with a cooked diet, it's necessary to ensure proper formula. Raw diets have downsides as well as rewards, and may not be ideal for every dog.

Caution

Many vets, while recognizing that pet food recalls and the low quality of some dog foods brings about concern, still believe that homemade diets, when fed solely, may lead to dietary instability and vitamin/mineral deficiencies that could pose risks to dog health. As a result, if you decide to feed your pet a homemade diet, it is crucial that you comprehend and supply what your dog needs to remain healthy; vet nutritionists can help in creating appropriate homemade diets. While extreme care was given to provide safe recommendations and precise instructions in this chapter, it's not possible to calculate an individual dog's response to any food or ingredient. You should consult your vet and make use of personal judgment when employing this information to your own dogs' diets.

CHAPTER FOUR

Homemade Dog Food and Treats Recipes

Several ready-made dry dog foods, commonly known as kibble, is stuffed with toxins, carcinogens, allergens and components that present your dog with inadequate base nourishment. Converting your pet from commercially produced, highly processed kibble to homemade dog food eater can be of significant advantage to your pet's general health.

Homemade dog food is arguably healthier than the ready-made dog food you can find in the supermarket, pet stores and vet clinics. Making your own dog food, however, take a little more time, but you can make extra and store it in the freezer.

Listed below are rather nutritious, easy to make dog food recipes that you can prepare and cook for your dog. The ingredients used are chosen to aid your pet's overall wellness, boost his disease fighting capability, reduce the chance of cancer, aid oral health, and more. When buying the ingredients used in the recipes, you can choose if you want to go organic or otherwise; but even if you choose the latter, rest assured that the recipes are carefully created to be packed with the right, good nutrition every canine needs.

Homemade Dog Food Recipes

Beef and Vegetable Balls

Some canines prefer meaty treats over sweet ones. This recipe has hearty meat flavor andgood aroma that all dogs really enjoy.

You'll need:

- 2 6-ounce jars of organic beef and vegetable baby food
- 1 cup of whole-wheat flour (or white substitute)
- 2 cups of dry milk
- 1 cup of waterInstructions:

1. Preheat the oven to 350 degrees Fahrenheit.
2. Combine all of the ingredients in a large mixing bowl.
3. Drop the mixture onto a baking sheet in large spoonfuls.
4. Bake for 12 to 15 minutes.

5. Allow to the treats to cool completely.

6. Store leftover beef and vegetable balls in the fridge for up to five days.

Turkey and Veggie Dinner

This basic dog food recipe incorporates turkey for protein and veggies for added vitaminsand minerals.

You'll need:

- 4 cups of water
- 1 pound of ground turkey
- 2 cups of brown rice
- 1 cup of carrots, chopped
- 1 cup of green beans, chopped
- 1 tablespoon of fish oil (optional)Instructions:

1. Cook the ground turkey in a non-stick skillet over medium heat until the meat iscooked through.

2. Add the brown rice, turkey, and water to a large pot and bring to a boil.

3. Reduce the heat to medium-low and cook an additional 15 minutes, or until the rice issoft and tender.

4. Add the carrots and green beans and cook for an additional 5 to 10 minutes, until thevegetables are tender.

5. Allow to cool before serving.//
6. Store extra dinners in the fridge for up to five days.

Chicken Casserole

This recipe utilizes chicken, which is a good source of protein, and plenty of vegetables to produce a flavorful mix. Green beans aid your dog feel full and veggies provide vitamins and minerals.

You'll need:

- 4 chicken breasts
- 1/2 cup of green beans, chopped
- 1/2 cup of carrots, chopped
- 1/2 cup of broccoli, chopped
- 1/2 cup rolled oats.
- 4 cups of low-salt chicken brothInstructions:

1. Take out excess fat from the chicken breasts and slice the breasts into small chunks.

2. Cook the chicken breasts in a non-stick skillet over medium heat until no longer pink.

3. Add the chicken, vegetables, rolled oats, and chicken broth to a large pot and cookover medium heat until the carrots are tender - about 15 minutes.

4. Allow to cool before serving.

5. Store leftover casserole portions in the fridge for up to five days.

Doggie Chili

Canines require considerable amounts of protein to ensure that they're healthy and active. Your puppy ought to get the majority of his protein from whole meat resources, like fresh chicken. Beans have a great amount of protein as well.

You'll need:

- 4 chicken breasts
- 1 cup of kidney beans, drained
- 1 cup of black beans, drained
- 1 cup of carrots, diced
- 1/2 cup of tomato paste
- 4 cups of chicken brothInstructions:

1. Take out the excess fat and dice the chicken breasts into small pieces.

2. Cook the chicken breasts in a non-stick skillet over medium-high heat until no longerpink.

3. Add the chicken, beans, carrots, tomato paste, and chicken broth into a large pot and cook over medium heat until heated through - about 10 minutes.

4. Allow the mixture to cool before serving.

5. Store leftover chili in the fridge for up to five days.

Homemade Dog Treats

Peanut Butter Cookies

Canines love peanut butter, and these cookies are a fantastic way to slip some fish oil into your pet's diet. This particular oil enhances your dog's coat, rendering it softer and healthier. For this recipe, it's recommended to use organic peanut butter since a number of commercial brands of peanut butter have unfit hydrogenated oils and preservatives. If you can't find an organic one, then just make your own! For this you'll only need raw peanuts and peanut oil (and a blender or food processor).

You'll need:

- 2 cups of flour (wheat if your pooch isn't allergic to it; white if he is)
- 1 cup of rolled oats

- 1/3 cup of smooth peanut butter
- 1 tablespoon of honey
- 1/2 tablespoon of fish oil
- 1 1/2 cups of waterInstructions:

1. Pre-heat the oven to 350 degrees Fahrenheit.

2. Combine the flour and oats together in a large mixing bowl. Pour in one cup of water and mix until smooth. Incorporate the peanut butter, honey, and fish oil and blend until all the ingredients are well combined.

3. Gradually add the water till the concoction has a thick and doughy consistency.

4. Mildly flour a cooking surface. Roll the dough onto the surface to make a 1/4 inchthick sheet.

5. Make use of a cookie cutter to make shapes. Put the cookies onto a baking sheet andbake for 40 minutes.

6. Let the cookies cool completely before feeding.

Chicken Jerky

The jerky is both tough and chewy, so it'll keep your dog entertained for some time. The chicken offers a beneficial amount of protein. Additionally, this treat can also help to clean the dog's teeth.

You'll need:

- Two to four chicken breastsInstructions:

1. Pre-heat the oven to 200 degrees Fahrenheit.
2. Get rid of any excess fat from the chicken. Turn the white meat on its side and use aparing knife to cut and portion the breast into 1/8 inch thick strips.
3. Set the strips on a baking sheet. Bake for two hours.
4. Test the chicken before removing from the oven. It must be dry and hard. Allow the chicken to cool completely before serving.
5. Store the jerky treat in an airtight jar/container inside the fridge. You can serve this toyour dog up to two weeks.

Frozen Yogurt Pops

This cool homemade treat is made out of human grade ingredients and contains fruit juice and carrots, which provide your four-legged friend an extra vitamin boost. Yogurt has calcium and protein, and helps your pet break down food.

You'll need:

- 6 oz. container of plain, NON-FAT frozen yogurt
- 1 cup of "no-sugar added" fruit juice
- 1/2 cup of carrots, mincedInstructions:

1. Add the yogurt, fruit juice, and carrots into a bowl. Mix until the ingredients aresmooth and well-blended.
2. Put the mixture into the ice cube trays.
3. Freeze until the mixtures are solid.

Fruit and Veggie Strips

These strips work as a more affordable substitute for the organic chewy treats available in pet stores. Additionally, they break apart effortlessly, so you can serve tinier pieces as training rewards. Fruit and veggies are abundant with vitamin C, which can boost your dog's body's defense mechanisms.

You'll need:
- 1 small sweet potato
- 1 medium banana
- 1 cup carrots, minced
- 1/2 cup unsweetened organic applesauce
- 2 cups of whole wheat flour (white if your pooch is allergic to wheat)
- 1 cup of rolled oats
- 1/3 cup of waterInstructions:

1. Cook the sweet potato in the microwave for 8 to 10 minutes, or until the insides are soft. Set aside and allow cooling.

2. Preheat the oven to 350 degrees Fahrenheit.

3. Mash the banana and sweet potato in a large mixing bowl with a hand masher until smooth. Incorporate the carrots, flour, and oats. Gradually add in the applesauce and water while mixing.

4. The ingredients will form soft dough. Roll the dough on to a lightly floured surface until its 1/8 inch thick.

5. Cut the dough into strips.

6. Cook on a baking sheet for 25 minutes.

7. Store leftover strips in the fridge for up to two weeks.

While many dogs can deal with a range of different treats given in small amounts, some may get indigestion if you switch foods too soon or excessively. Prior to starting making your own homemade dog food, speak with your vet and ask if he / she has any specific ingredient recommendations, as some dog breeds may be more susceptible to food allergies than others. After acquiring your vet's approval, change your dog's food over little by little, slowing blending in a homemade dish with your regular food for a coupleof days to a week.

CHAPTER FIVE

Food Dogs Can and Can't Eat

When you see your dog giving you a sad little look while standing near the dinner table, you could be inclined to slip your furry friend a bit of your food. Sharing food with your dog may appear fairly harmless, but beyond stimulating bad begging habits and even putting on weight, you could essentially be putting your dog's general health and life in danger.

There are a variety of foods and ingredients eaten by humans daily, such as chocolate, milk and garlic that can induce severe toxic reactions in pets. In this chapter, we're going to take particular notice at the ones that can be most hazardous to your four-legged pal.

Safe Human Foods for Dogs

There are human food items that are acceptable to feed to your dog; even so, these items must be kept as small as possible. These food items are:

Lean Meat - Lean meat consists of meat devoid of bones that has had the extra fat taken off. If feeding chicken and turkey, the skin must also be removed as it can be a source of fat. Lean meat includes the white meat from chicken or turkey and offers a tasty treat for your doggie in addition to a superior source of protein.

Raw (and cooked) Eggs - The most apparent problem here is salmonella, but raw diet fanatics promote the effectiveness of a raw egg in your dog's diet. While the white provides the Avidin enzyme, which prevents the absorption of vitamin B (Biotin), the yolk contains more than sufficient Biotin to balance out the enzyme. So, when fed raw and whole, or cooked and whole, eggs are loaded with protein and a host of natural vitamins for your dog.

Fruits - Dogs can safely savor bananas, apple slices, strawberries, blueberries and watermelon. The seeds must be taken off these fruits or in the case of watermelon it hasto be a seedless one as most fruit seeds have arsenic that is poisonous. Fresh fruits are an excellent treat to help in training your dog and can likewise provide your pet with a good way to cool down during summer days.

Vegetables - Selected veggies like carrots, green beans, cucumber slices or zucchini slices all are excellent treats for your dog. It's smart to replace commercial dog treats with baby carrots if you want to slim your dog down a bit. Veggies make great low- calorie treats and good training tools too. But steer clear of canned and pickled vegetables since they have excessive salt.

Baked potatoes - A plain baked potato is fine to feed your dog but in all honesty it's not something that ought to be done regularly and must never include any toppings. A few pieces of cooked baked potato can be a great treat for a patient puppy.

White Rice and Pasta - White rice and pasta are often termed as a potential meal for a dog with indigestion. Normally boiled white chicken and white rice are utilized to help firm up stools along with nurture a dog that is having difficulty getting any nutrition from food because of illness.

While there are definitely some human foods that are safe to give your dog, there are numerous which are hazardous and potentially poisonous when consumed by your pet. Generally speaking, it's best to be safe than sorry so steer clear of feeding your dog any human food unless of course suggested by your vet.

Dogs that aren't given human food or table scraps are often better behaved than dogs who do get people food anyway, they don't beg since they know they won't get any scraps and they also have a tendency to drool less and hassle visitors to your home less given that they understand that human food is for people and not for them.

Unsafe Human Food for Dogs

Alcohol - Alcohol can result in not just intoxication, loss of coordination, poor breathing, and irregular acidity, but possibly even coma and/or death.

Apple Seeds - Apple seeds are harmful to a dog as they contain a natural chemical that releases cyanide when consumed. So, make sure to core and seed apples before you give them to your pooch.

Avocado - Avocados have Persin, which can cause diarrhea, nausea, and heart congestion.

Baby food - Baby food alone isn't bad, just make sure it doesn't contain any kind of onion powder. Baby food also doesn't have all the nutrients a dog depends on for a healthy, well kept diet.

Bones - The risk with bones isn't the dietary content, nor is it always the danger of chocking. Instead, you have to be careful with bones from meat sources like chicken and fish since they may damage your dog's digestive tract once the bones splinter inside the body.

Candy and Gum - Besides candy contain sugar; it often has Xylitol, which can result in the over-release of insulin, kidney failure, and worse, death.

Cat food - Not that the dog would want this at any rate, but cat food has proteins and fats which are directed at the diet of a cat, NOT a dog. The protein and fat levels in cat food are far too high for your pooch, thus rendering it unhealthy for dogs.

Chocolate - You've probably heard this before, but chocolate is a DEFINITE NO-NO for dogs. And it's not only about caffeine, which is more than enough to cause harm to your dog alone, but theobromine and theophylline, which is usually toxic, result in panting, vomiting, and diarrhea, and impair your dog's heart and nervous systems.

Citrus Oil Extracts - Leads to vomiting.

Coffee - The information and rules here are pretty much the same with the info and rules against chocolate. This is basically poison for your dog if consumed.

Corn on the cob - This is a guaranteed method of getting your dog's intestine obstructed. The corn is digested, but the cob gets stuck in the small intestine, and if it's not taken out surgically, can be fatal to your dog. Furthermore, excessive corn kernels can distressed the digestive tract too.

Fat trimmings - Leads to pancreatitis.

Fish - The principal fish you need to be cautious of are salmon and trout. Raw salmon can be deadly to dogs if the fish is contaminated with a certain parasite, Nanophyetus salmincola. The parasite by itself isn't harmful to dogs, but is usually infected with bacteria called Neorickettsia helminthoeca, which oftentimes is lethal to canines if not dealt with correctly. However, cooked salmon is okay as it kills the parasite.

Grapes and Raisins - This is one that a number of dog owners do not know. Grapes have a toxin that leads to severe liver damage and kidney failure.

Human vitamins - Some human vitamins are acceptable to use, but the important thing is assessing the ingredients (every one of them - active and inactive) to the vitamins your vet registers for your dog. Make certain there's no iron, as this can harm the digestive system lining, and turn out to be toxic for the liver and kidneys.

Liver - Prevent feeding too much liver to your pooch. Liver contains a substantial amount of Vitamin A, which can detrimentally affect your pup's muscles and bones.

Macadamia nuts - These have a toxin that can slow down locomotory activities, leading to weakness, panting, swollen limbs, and tremors along with possible injury to your dog's digestive, nervous, and muscle systems.

Milk and Dairy Products - While small doses aren't likely to kill your dog, you might get some smelly farts and some awful cases of diarrhea. Why? Dogs are lactose- intolerant, and don't have sufficient of the lactase enzyme to effectively digest dairy foods. If you need to give them dairy, consider lactose-free products.

Mushrooms - Just like the wrong mushroom can be deadly to humans, the same pertains to dogs.

Onions, Garlic, and Chives - Regardless of what form they're in (dry, raw, cooked, powder, within other foods), onions and garlic (particularly onions) are among the absolute worst foods you may give your pup. These are poison to canines. They contain disulfides and sulfoxides (thiosulphate), both can cause anemia and destroy red blood cells.

Persimmons, Peaches, and Plums - If you reside in an area that is home to persimmon, peach, or plum trees, watch out. Persimmon seeds and peach and plum pits leads to intestinal obstruction and enteritis. You need to ensure there aren't any wild persimmon or other fruit trees that leave seeds growing in your backyard.

Rhubarb and Tomato leaves - These contain oxalates that can detrimentally impact the digestive, nervous, and urinary systems.

Raw fish - Yet another vitamin B (Thiamine) deficit might result from the regular ingestion of raw fish. Appetite loss will be prevalent, accompanied by seizures, and in exceptional instances, death.

Salt - Much like salt isn't the healthiest item for people, it's much less healthy for canines. An excessive amount of it can result in an imbalance in electrolyte levels, dehydration and possibly diarrhea.

Sugar - This is applicable to any food that contains sugar. Make sure you confirm the ingredient label for human foods - corn syrup can be found in just about everything nowadays. An excessive amount of sugar for your dog can result in dental issues, obesity,and sometimes diabetes.

Tobacco - A primary toxic hazard for canines. The consequences nicotine has on dogs are considerably worse than on humans. Nicotine damages your pup's digestive and nervous systems, boost their heart rate, make them faint, and eventually lead to death.

Xylitol - A sugar alcohol present in gum, candies, baked goods, and other sugar- substituted products, Xylitol, while triggering no apparent injury to humans, is incredibly toxic to canines. Even a small amount leads to low blood sugar, convulsions, liver failure,even fatality for your pooch.

Yeast (by itself or in dough) - Much like yeast rises in bread, it will likewise expand and rise inside your pup's tummy. Make certain they don't get any. While mild cases will result in gas, plenty of farting, and distress - an excessive amount of it may rupture their stomach and intestines.

Keep These Out Of Your Dog's Reach Too

While these don't necessarily fall under a specific class above, you will want to stay away from them too:

- **Old food** - You never like old and moldy food, so what on earth makes you think your pet will? The bacteria in spoiled food is made up of all sorts of toxins that is usually damaging to your dog's health. Give them the freshest and best, dog-approved food only.

- **Leftovers** - If you feed them leftovers frequently they will not receive a proper diet. If you do give them table scraps, always remove any bones and trim down the fat.

- **Examine the ingredients** - Final point here is making sure to know what's in the food your giving your pet. The food items abovementioned should undoubtedly NOT be on there. You'd be amazed at the number of foods contain sugar and caffeine, that you simply wouldn't expect to without first checking the ingredient list.

- **Human treats** - Chips can have garlic and onion powder, cookies may have raisins, chocolate or macadamia nuts.

Bottom line - there is a reason there's food and treats made particularly for dogs.

When In Doubt, Ask the Vet

If your pooch is behaving oddly, or suffering from even minor signs such as weakness, lack of coordination, nausea, diarrhea, etc. and you think he may have eaten something he shouldn't have, go to the vet right away. If you wait a long time, your pet may not makeit.

CONCLUSION

Not a lot of canine owners go for homemade dog food, possibly since they don't have enough time to do this. Most people feed their dogs canned food and/or dry food which come in a bag. While there are particular table foods that unquestionably aren't healthy for dogs, providing them with food you make at home isn't a problem, too. The simple truth is you may enhance the nutrition that your dog gets once you begin managing the food making process.

The advantage of homemade dog food is that you can be certain that the ingredients are well-balanced and healthy for your pet. It's simple to find quality recipes to concoct a good dog food that will boost your pet's health. So, what makes homemade dog food healthier and better than store-bought ones?

- One of the principal benefits of making time and effort to create homemade dog food for your dog is that you'll be sure that he gets fresh produce. You don't have to be worried about the food being expired or polluted.
- One more of the benefits you'll like if you start cooking homemade dog food instead of buying commercial ones is affordability. You'll discover that manufactured dog foods can get fairly pricey. Those processed foods particularly can take up your cash easily. Creating your own dog food is more cost-effective generally, while still offering quality ingredients and good nutrition to your dog.
- There's numerous dog food recipes offered online and by your vet you can make at home. You don't need to present your dog the usual food all the time. Let him enjoy various flavors often, which keeps him acquiring a variety of nutrition too.

Essentially, you'll find surely a number of exceptional good things about homemade dog food. Sure, it should take quite a while for you to prepare and make the food, but your dog will make it worthwhile.

***